$\mathcal{P}$resented to:

Tim

From:

Dad ; mom

Date:

8/18/3

A BOOK OF HOPE

for
Students

DREAM BIG! DREAM WISELY!

written by ... Debbie Guthery
edited by ... Kathy Knight, Alecia Harper & Cecil O. Kemp, Jr.

written by ...
Debbie Guthery

A very, very special thanks to ...
Stephen von Hagel, Robert Kiefer and Brenda McClearen. Stephen had the idea for The Hope Collection and shepherded the creative effort, working closely with Robert, Brenda and their associates.

edited by ...
Kathy Knight, Alecia Harper & Cecil O. Kemp, Jr.

Art Direction ...
McClearen Design Studios
3901 Brush Hill Rd.   Nashville, TN 37216   615-859-4550

To Reach the Author and Publisher ...
The Wisdom Company, Inc.
P. O. Box 681351   Franklin, TN 37068-1351
1-615-791-7186

About The Hope Collection –

Each Hope Collection book is based on Cecil O. Kemp, Jr's acclaimed inspirational book, **Wisdom Honor & Hope**.

Hope—without it, no one can live very long.
No great conquests have ever been won without it.
No one has ever seen better days without hoping for them.
Nurture hope and it will reward you.
Hope is the sunshine of life and the angel that puts a song
in your heart.
What gives you hope?
The authors and publishers invite you to enjoy this and other Hope Collection Gift Books.

About the Creator of The Hope Collection –

Cecil O. Kemp, Jr. lived his dream, becoming a successful businessman and business owner. Yet, he was very unfulfilled. Enormous material success didn't deliver on its promises of hope and happiness. He set out to discover the secrets of a genuinely happy, hopeful life. Finding and applying them, he freed himself and his family from the rat race life, while enjoying even greater material success. After nearly two decades of this higher prosperity, he offers those amazing discoveries in The Hope Collection. Kemp and other Hope Collection writers invite readers to begin their own journey of the heart toward real and lasting peace, hope, happiness and success.

Introduction

There is a time in our lives when we begin to question our direction. My mother used to call that time the "awakening of our souls."

If we listen closely to what our heart is telling us, we will sense the direction—the destiny—that has been meant for us all along.

It is only then that we can open ourselves to Dream Big—allowing ourselves to accept as reality the passions and desires in our soul.

If our dreams are honorable and spiritually born, then we Dream Wisely, ensuring our success if we continue to allow God's partnership along our path.

At every step we must remember to Breathe. We must take time to meditate, regroup, reflect, savor life's pleasure and pain, ask for God's inspiration, and willingly inspire others.

This is the course to Wisdom and Fulfillment.

This is the path to Freedom.

Dedication

This book is dedicated to my father, who gave me a strong foundation to build upon and to my mother who gave me an opened window with a view of possibilities, to the light of my life, my son Tyler, the honest heart of my husband Barry and for the wisdom and guidance of a wonderful teacher Cecil Kemp, Jr.

Faith is a powerful gift, always believe for that is where miracles begin.

Thanks, Steve for believing in me.

To my wonderful editor Kathryn Knight who took my words and strengthened their *meaning*, you heard my heart's whisper.

–*Debbie Guthrey*

Dream ***Big...***

Passion
  is the wind beneath our wings
and the storm that
  takes our breath away.
-Debbie Guthery

Dreams

The best way to make your *dreams*
come true is to *wake up*.
—Paul Valéry

The masterpieces of life lie in the hearts of so many people who are waiting to breathe, waiting to soar, waiting to be.

Dreams give us wings and bring us peace. Each of us has a dream. It may be modest, it may be all-consuming, but it is there—seed, a hope, a desire, a breath. Reach inside yourself and dare to open your heart. Discover your wings, stretch them, move them and learn how to use them to fly.

With faith by your side, possibilities in your heart, and the sky within your reach, you can do anything!

miracle waiting to be b

🌑 **Nugget** of **Hope**
Inside each heart lies a miracle waiting to be born, and oh, how heaven's chimes will ring then!

Doubt

Doubt is the **vestibule** which *all must pass before* they can enter the temple of wisdom.
—Colton

Every little doubt, every little worry is our own illusion of failure. And we are afraid to fail. That fear comes from the unknown—that creature that lives behind so many doors, hides in mysterious boxes, filling our thoughts with fear and doubt, binding us to inaction.

Don't let doubt stall your dreams. Harness that which is achievable and shed the bridle that leads you nowhere.

Doubt crops up in the face of decision, perhaps even change, which can be accompanied by discomfort—a normal reaction. But if we look back in our lives at the times we were uncomfortable, we will notice that often those were times when we grew—when we experienced "growing pains"—even if it was a time of "failure."

Failures are not endings. They are guides that tell us something didn't work the way we planned. A failure creates the perfect opportunity to dust yourself off and try again.

We can only achieve our dreams if we recognize and cast off our doubts, accept the unknown, learn from our "failures" and stay on the course we've set for ourselves.

Nugget of Hope
Faith and hope are our heart's eyes and higher intellect, the spiritual vision and knowledge that drive fear from our spirits as we soar beyond doubt.

—Cecil O. Kemp, Jr.

Faith

By believing in roses, **one brings them to bloom.**

—French proverb

Bright are her eyes my little girl Faith

her timing soft her presence like lace

She appears in a whisper as one believes

and captures a moment sometimes hard to conceive.

She clears all the darkness that hides passion's light

and shows us a way through the darkest nights

So subtle her spirit, so strong is her hold

believing is simple with Faith to behold.

If you believe, you will see. Let faith guide you and show the brightest of all lights. Lay down the weapons protecting your heart and trust in your spirit to fly.

Nugget of Hope

Picture the beauty of roses in faith. Wisdom plants them, Honor waters them, and Hope comes back, soaks in, and enjoys their beauty and fragrance.

—Cecil O. Kemp, Jr.

Time

Time is a wave, which never murmurs, because there is no obstacle to its flow.

—Mme. Swetchine

I don't have enough…

I'm going to run out of…

I wish I had more…

What words did you automatically put in those blanks?

We tend to measure our lives in time; "Time will heal all wounds," and "Oh, the pains of time." I'm late, it's late, they're late; tomorrow, today, yesterday, now. Time is so important to us because we think we don't have enough, it's going to run out, and we wish we had more. We spend more time worrying about running out of time than we do running with it.

Time triggers an illusion of limits. But time goes on with or without us, therefore it is limitless. If it is limitless, there will always be enough to go around, and it's never going to run out. You can change your concept of time. You can choose to think instead:

I do have enough time.

I'm going to run with time.

I have more time than I'll ever need.

Time gives, time takes; time is the river that sees no end and hears no cries. It comes and goes, but forever flows. It will continue its flow whether we wish it away or wish for more, so we must enjoy its essence and ride its current.

Nugget of Hope

Our life is a currency we spend only once. Spend it wisely, but be reckless giving your love.

—Cecil O. Kemp, Jr.

Permission

If we fail to dream, we die.
—Sigmund Freud

When we dream, we turn off the lights, cover ourselves up, and fade off into a world where our imagination steers us to fantastic places. Here we release our anxieties, face our fears, uncover our fantasies, and bare our souls. There is no price to pay; there are no rules to follow, no final destination. There is no permission to seek—or none is required.

When we awake we begin our days dressing for someone else, doing for someone else, and often living for someone else. No wonder we are geared toward asking for permission, or making sure that what we do is within "policy guidelines." Of course, some rules are necessary to keep us safe, but don't we also tend to self-impose rules on ourselves?

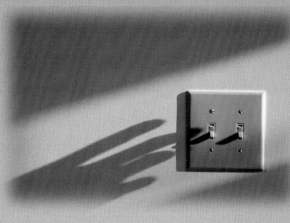

Here are some things to think about...

- Is it all right to cry over spilled milk? to be angry about a situation you're not happy with? to laugh in church? to hug a stranger?

- Is it okay to dream?

- I ask myself, can I grow? Whisper yes, as faith does flow!

⊙ **N**ugget of **H**ope
On the inner path of Wisdom, Honor and Hope you have the inspiration, power, passion and permission to pursue highest dreams and true greatness.
—*C e c i l O . K e m p , J r .*

Denial

No man remains quite what he was when he recognizes himself.

—Thomas Mann

Denial is a blindfold to our pain. It is much easier to cover our eyes than to face pain. If we face up to our decisions or problems, we can resolve them through faith and wise action. Denial is the shadow that lies beneath the wind.

We all know people in denial. Those who cannot admit that they overdrink, that their relationship is truly over, that their child's disturbing behavior is not normal, that their terminally ill loved one will not fully recover. These are very easy to pick out as cases of denial, misplaced hope, protection from pain.

But one of the most inhibiting forms of denial we can face as spiritual beings lies deeper. It is refusing to believe—refusing to see and know—that our dreams can be real (and must become real) if we hope to live fully, pleasing ourselves and God.

When you say, "I just can't go follow my soul's desire" aren't you in denial to the power you possess with the help of your Creator?

Uncover your eyes to view the bigger picture of your destiny. Recognize yourself. Believe.

Nugget of Hope
Denial is accepting and living untruths.
We can know the Truth and be free!

—*Cecil O. Kemp, Jr.*

Acceptance

> **Condemnation** does not
> liberate, it **oppresses**.
> —Carl Jung

We see things in ourselves that very few others see. We pick out every flaw in our faces, every little freckle on our bodies, every little imperfection, and magnify them in our minds. Then we criticize, improvise and modify so that these very unimportant flaws become ridiculous burdens that we try to hide, fix or change. We oppress ourselves with our lack of self-acceptance—

we are critical of the dreamer. And if we don't accept the dreamer, how are we to believe in the dreams?

When you see imperfections in your reflection, handle them with care.

There are so many situations in our lives that seem to throw us off track—divorce, death, illness, failures, and denial, for example. These things directly affect how we perceive ourselves and others, and our immediate response may be to feel shame, or to regret, condemn and try to "change" them. But it is important that we accept and free ourselves—to see conditions for what they are, acknowledge how we feel about them, make amends, and go on with our lives, holding close to our hearts what we have learned. We become stronger from our experiences. We become wiser with our acceptance.

Nugget of Hope
Freedom arrives the moment we admit that life's tough and we're not perfect.

—*Cecil O. Kemp, Jr.*

FEAR

When you have collected all the facts and fears and made your decision, turn off all your fears and go ahead.
—Gen. George S. Patton, Jr.

Sometimes we let fear establish how we act, who we are, and how we are supposed to be. When we are surrounded by fear—the fear society feels—and feel it within ourselves, we may run to our corners and refuse to come out. But there is hope. We can recognize that fear does exist—it is real—but can be surmounted.

My grandfather came to the United States in the late 1930's after escaping from a German prison camp. He was faced with the very real fear of starting life in a new country with only $5 in his pocket. He could have felt overwhelmed with this fear and his daunting situation. Instead, he decided to turn off the fear, assess his situation and make a plan and dare to dream big. He went on to become a successful New York attorney! He chose not to dwell on what he had lost, and he did not stand still in his fear. He took what he had and jumped back into life. Fear can motivate us to act, if we face it head-on.

Life is not meant to be lived cowering in the corner. It is meant to be challenged and explored. Acknowledge fear's reality, but then leap from fear's grasp.

Nugget of Hope

Say good-bye to your fears and welcome Wisdom's Motive into your heart, with open arms!

—*Cecil O. Kemp, Jr.*

Security

The climate of truth is not inclement; it is clear and temperate and perfectly fair. We weather well in such a climate.

—Grace McFarland

We have fences to protect our properties, locks to protect our homes and meteorologists to tell us there is a good chance of rain.

We spend a great deal of time, money and effort to assure ourselves of protection and safety from circumstances

experience unbelievable things, see incredible sigl

that may throw us off kilter or take us by surprise. We stay with a job that drains our spirit—just because it's safer than daring to dream and explore. We forego journeys, adventures, expressing our feelings, trying our wings, living our dreams—all in the name of security.

But the truth is that security and the "status quo" can not really be guaranteed. You are wise to take safe measures, but you were not put on this earth to spend your life ensuring your comfort. Don't let a forecast of rain stop you! Dream big! Have a grand adventure! Maybe you'll get a little wet or hurt, maybe you won't be safe from life's "slings and arrows," but you will be truly living.

Experience unbelievable things, see incredible sights, and learn that there are very few limits to your dreams. By the way, there's a good chance of sunshine today.

Nugget of Hope
The beginning of anxiety is the end of faith, and the beginning of true faith is the end of anxiety.

—George Mueller

nd learn that there are very few limits to your dre

Procrastination

Tomorrow is often the busiest day of the week. —*Spanish proverb*

The task at hand is often the motivation to do easier tasks that could wait. When we are faced with a life changing decision or even initiating our heart's dream, we often find plenty of things that "need" our attention at the same time.

The most difficult step to take to begin the journey toward a dream can be the first—simply to start—simply to commit to a beginning. Ask yourself, "If I put this off until tomorrow, how will I feel about myself when I wake up? If I put this off until next week, how will I feel in a week? If I put this off for another year—to do other chores, fulfill a variety of obligations—how will I feel this time next year?

When we procrastinate, we are generally running from fear, anxiety, lack of knowledge or frustration. These are real feelings and should be acknowledged as such—but they do nothing to propel us toward our dreams.

Now is the time to begin. Today shall always be; yesterday

and tomorrow are merely whispers of changing seasons.

Procrastination limits our flight. Cut the ropes—dare the skies!

 **N**ugget of **H**ope

Procrastination is a nightmare habit! Choose wise action instead!

-Cecil O. Kemp, Jr.

Achievement

Aim high. **Success lies** *not in achieving what you aim at, but* **in aiming** *at what you ought to achieve.*

—R.F. Horton

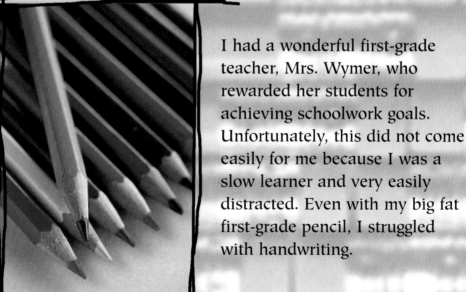

I had a wonderful first-grade teacher, Mrs. Wymer, who rewarded her students for achieving schoolwork goals. Unfortunately, this did not come easily for me because I was a slow learner and very easily distracted. Even with my big fat first-grade pencil, I struggled with handwriting.

As the whole class drilled, practiced and improved, the "Thin Pencil Fairy" would come and leave thin pencils in Mrs. Wymer's desk with names on them of students who had perfected their letters (as well as first-graders could!).

The school year flew by and the Thin Pencil Fairy still had not left me a thin pencil. I decided I would work as hard as I could at making my letters perfect. I worked at home and at recess. Barely two weeks before summer break, Mrs. Wymer announced that the Thin Pencil Fairy had left a thin pencil for... Debbie. I had done it! I still have the pencil to prove to myself how wonderful achievement can be.

After you climb one mountain, no matter how small, you may find that the rest are easier to conquer. So take a deep breath, reach high, and latch onto the stars. Then glance upon the riches of accomplishment.

🌑 **N**ugget of **H**ope
We are successful when we surrender self to God.
—*C e c i l   O .   K e m p ,   J r .*

Passion

True *passion* is not a wisp-light;
it is a *consuming flame*
and either it must find fruition
or it *will burn the human
heart* to dust and ashes.
—William Winter

Passion is the wildfire in our hearts that, when unchained, can determine our direction.

If you were arrested for being passionate about your desires and interests, would there be enough evidence to convict you? Never, _never_ tell yourself that your dream—the desire that God shares with you—is too minor, too small, or too insignificant not to warrant your passion! Put gusto, commitment and joy into your heart's work whatever it may be. Every idea that is explored, every question that is answered, every creative impulse that is put into action adds to life—not just yours, but to all of life.

There is absolutely nothing "selfish" about being passionate about your dreams. In fact, when you deny this burning desire, you deny the world the benefit of your talent, your work and your ideas.

● **N**ugget of **H**ope
Divine purpose comes alive inside,
as the passion of our life.

—*Cecil O. Kemp, Jr.*

Limitations

The person who is limited in heart and thought is inclined to love that which is limited in life, and the weak sighted cannot see more than one cubit ahead upon the path he treads, nor more than one cubit of the wall upon which he rests his shoulder.

—Kahlil Gibran

My nine-year-old son is wonderful to watch in a room full of objects. He has the ability to create "masterpieces" (in my estimation) very quickly. There are no limits to his imagination; he doesn't admit the concept of limits.

As we grow, we are taught—and

choose to accept—limits that can bind us.

We tell ourselves that we are limited by our education, money, time, talent, appearance, resources, experience, handicaps, age, race, gender—the list can go on. By accepting and believing in limitations we do more than construct obstacles to achieving our goals and dreams. We allow a mind set that limits our very thoughts—our very ability to open ourselves to dreaming—and our lives actually do become limited. Our light becomes hidden in deceptions. We then find it difficult to clear the thorn bushes in our way and find our path again.

We need to remember the child within us. The child who scaled his crib, the child who dared to color outside the lines, the child who railed against limitations or quietly asked "Why not?" Because of my son, I realize my own limitless potential. I asked him one day, "Where did you get all that talent?" He replied "From your stomach."

Follow your heart and believe!

Nugget of Hope
Stand nose to nose with a brick wall and see nothing; climb to the top and jump into anything!
—Debbie Guthery

Vision

Veni. Vidi. Vici.

—Julius Caesar, 47 B.C.,
translated: I came. I saw. I conquered.

Caesar's victory over Pontus, Pharnaces II, began before the battle—it began with his vision of victory. Vision is a pure conception of what we see for our lives. In a "realistic" light, limits can surround our dreams. However, if we can believe that what we envision is truly real, our limitations quickly vanish and our dreams become reality.

When I divorced, I lost everything—my house, my job, my financial security, and my self-confidence. I was truly humbled. After endless tears, I decided I was capable of getting on my feet, getting a good education, and getting a good job. I was on my way, but not quite there. I had a three year old son, I had not a dime to my name, and my schedule was inflexible.

I began writing in my journal, prayers of a sort, with my new resolves and visions for my future. As I read them at the end of each week, I "saw" what I needed—and things began to happen. I received a Pell grant to pay for my education, and I got a job at a local television station that encouraged and made time for my education. A friend told me about a preschool that catered to children my son's age. Obstacles to my path became fewer and fewer. I believe that the act of envisioning actually brought these circumstances my way.

Hold your dreams in the palms of your hands, and watch the possibilities flourish.

Nugget of Hope

When the Hope of Wisdom enters our hearts, our inner vision turns every day, even stormy or "dog" days, to brighter, better days, full of sunshine.

—Cecil O. Kemp, Jr.

Creation

A blank surface — the wall of a museum, a canvas, or an empty page in a typewriter —
can be daunting. Then when you start out doing something, creating, the beginning strikes awe within you.

—Edward Steichen

We are creative spirits. In fact, it is our duty to find within us what we are to create and offer the world. Your dreams are not merely wishes - they are callings. A creative task can be very difficult—even scary—but the rewards are a joyful communion between God and your own soul and a gift you can share with others.

I was asked to write a paper about death for my creative writing class after a classmate, a dear friend, was killed. My teacher felt that we needed to address the situation, grieve, and go on with our lives.

The assignment was difficult because I had feelings I had not experienced before and did not know how to express. I became anxious about facing that challenge. It wasn't until I had written everything except the assignment that I realized I would have to do it or accept a failing grade. I finally started at midnight, and the words wondrously flowed from me, creating one of my very best papers. What I had feared, what my teacher had asked of me—to write from and with emotion—turned out to be what I now appreciate and trust as a gift.

Release the special talent within you—trust this and fly.

Nugget of Hope
The creative power within can bring abundance.
—*Cecil O. Kemp, Jr.*

Determination

The person who makes a success of living is the one who sees his goal steadily and aims for it unswervingly.
—Cecil B. DeMille

I have made up my mind to find the top of the world and savor its view.

I have a very close friend who was recently diagnosed with multiple sclerosis, or MS. She has always been extremely active and loves the outdoors. When the doctors told her she would eventually be limited in the activities she could do, she decided to conquer her greatest fear: water-skiing in the ocean. She felt if she didn't face her fear, she would never know if she had a reason to be fearful. So she tried, and she triumphed over her fear. MS has not yet slowed her down; perhaps that's because she believes she has so much more to do with her life, and her determination has postponed the progress of the disease.

Determination is one of the final steps we take before we board the ship of dreams. We can make a wise decision and focus on the effort to bring it to fruition. When you get to this point, let your determination handle the wheel. Then you will take a ride you will never forget.

Nugget of Hope
Determination is the inner rope that keeps us hanging in, taking us to the top of the mountains of success others long ago quit climbing.

—Cecil O. Kemp, Jr.

Motivation

Every blade of grass **has its angel**
that bends over it and whispers,
"Grow, grow."
—The Talmud

The thirst for our dreams is the reason we seek the fresh
waters of life. This thirst motivates us to go on, grow on,
dream on.

When we pursue our dreams, our motivations must
be clear. What is the motivation behind your
dream? It is imperative that you know. Are you
motivated by financial gain? Recognition?
Jealousy? Prestige? Or are you motivated by a
still, small voice that seems divinely inspired that
never ceases to whisper, "Grow, grow"?

To Dream Big is essential to success. But if your dreams are not wisely motivated, you will not experience the ultimate success your destiny holds—a life of Honor, Peace, Joy, Promise and Passion.

Wise motivation inspires us to take risks to seek out our true desires and helps us to distinguish the right direction to take. Wise motivation gives us the little push so many of us need to begin our dream journeys.

With clear minds, healthy bodies, and strong convictions, we can tune into our inner spiritual selves. Then our vision will be clear—we can find a new direction for our lives—we will see the direction in which to are meant to travel. All we need is to listen to the voice of motivation from within to push us confidently along.

Nugget of Hope
Wise motivation and choice are the on-ramps to the path to excellence and lasting success.

—*Cecil O. Kemp, Jr.*

Dream Wisely...

Wisdom continually points us upward, reminding us to discover and fulfill the eternal purpose of our lives.
—Cecil O. Kemp, Jr.

Wisdom

*Wisdom is the cornerstone
of the path to excellence and lasting success.
It magnifies our talents and illuminates
the path of life.
In its right hand is long
life, and in its left riches
and honor.*
—Cecil O. Kemp, Jr.

To know You is to love You,
   as I find my way to be.

And those who share my life
   will feel Your peace
   through me,

For this I vow upon my heart as long as I shall breathe.

His words are wise,

His paintings are divine,

His heart is filled with an abundance of love;

Thus find the Lord, Teacher of all dreams.

The dictionary defines wisdom as: the power or faculty of forming a sound judgment in any matter; sagacity; experience. The Bible defines wisdom throughout its readings as finding truths, about ourselves and about our direction. No matter how we pray, through meditation, or in the company of others, we are always blessed with answers to our questions that bring peace to our stressful lives.

Wisdom tells us it is important to keep sight of the road, to examine our heart knowledge, and to be true to who we are. We are children of God, created in His own image and kissed by the heavens above.

Nugget of Hope

As we connect with our faith, we discover our reason to be—and we approach Wisdom.

–Debbie Guthery

Desire

To drink is a small matter. To be thirsty is everything.
—Georges Duamel

Savor all that is put on your plate, and always ask for seconds.

Desire is the appetite for life. Just as we need nourishment for our bodies, we need our desires to feed our souls. Desires reveal our direction.

Breathe in the sweet fragrances and caress your visions.

If you were granted one—and only one—wish, what would it be?

King Midas desired to change everything he touched into gold. Well, eventually he did just that. Unfortunately, he touched his daughter and turned her into an exquisite work of art. King Midas learned a valuable lesson about desire—unwise desire, that is—and greed. If we desire and fight desperately to keep up with the Joneses or hunger for fame and fortune, we will lose our direction in life.

It is important that we make the distinction between unwise and wise desires. Wise desire often means sacrifice—wise desires do not always promise any easy path, but wise desires lead you to true abundance.

With this in mind, close your eyes and imagine you are in a place where you find comfort. Breathe in the sweet fragrances around you; caress your visions. Think about what you love about this place and listen carefully. You will hear a quiet whisper of the heart, a tiny piece of your dreams.

Nugget of Hope
True greatness begins by holding wise desires in our hearts.

—*Cecil O. Kemp, Jr.*

Purpose

Every man has his own destiny: the only imperative is to follow it, accept it, no matter where it leads.
—Henry Miller

When we are confident that we have dreamed wisely, we still encounter stumbling blocks that make us question, "Why is this in my way?" or "Why is this happening to me?" Stop and take a breath and ask instead, "What could be the purpose of this obstacle? What could this set-back teach me?"

When I committed to a goal of physical fitness I started working out with a personal trainer. The first workouts made me so sore I could barely get out of bed, let alone walk! I was losing motivation until my trainer assured me that the pain would pass and that it had a purpose-to teach me just how out-of-shape I was!

Each experience along your dream journey has a purpose. How more divine, then, must be the purpose for your being placed on this earth!

When your dreams are

wisely inspired and passion fills
your heart, you are living your
purpose. Stay on the path. The rest of us need you to live your destiny—in some way it will teach us, help us, touch us- your life—your dream-holds purpose in our lives.

Nugget of Hope
When our purpose is eternal in its aim, our priority in living and working is what has value in eternity.
— Cecil O. Kemp, Jr.

Opportunity

People are always blaming their circumstances for what they are. I don't believe in circumstances. The people who get on in this world are people who get up and look for the circumstances they want, and, if they can't find them, make them.
—George Bernard Shaw

Have you ever heard the old saying that opportunity knocks, but sometimes very quietly? I am a firm believer that every day is a new opportunity waiting to be discovered.

From Webster's dictionary we read: *Opportunity—a combination of circumstances favorable for the purpose*

. Think about that! If you have faith that your purpose is divinely inspired—in spiritual partnership—then surely you will encounter a "combination of circumstances favorable for the purpose." Opportunities abound when you are on the path of Wisdom, the path revealed by your dreams! You also have the power—the permission—to create the circumstances that bring you opportunities.

A friend of mine, who has the voice of an angel, moved to Nashville to pursue a career in the music industry. She would pound the pavement every day, knocking on doors and passing out demo tapes, but no one ever called. She decided to put a band together and play for fun. She now has a loving husband, two beautiful daughters, and a steady gig at her church.

Here's the real kicker: She has since been offered several recording contracts and turned all of them down. When we spoke about her career, I asked her why on earth she had turned down those opportunities. She smiled. "They have had their opportunity, and God found mine."

Nugget of Hope
Let the Spirit of God within guide you to new heights pursuing life's best opportunities.

—*Cecil O. Kemp, Jr.*

Getting to Work

That's the reason so many dreamers fail—they're not willing to come down out of the clouds and get to work at the things that turn their stomachs.

—Susan Glaspell

Ready...

You've opened your heart to dreaming big!

Set...

You've examined your desires and motivations in order to dream wisely!

Go!!

What do you mean you're catching your breath?

In the dizzying atmosphere where we fly with passion under our wings, we can easily become lightheaded, caught up in the wonder of spiritual connectedness. In a sense, we must leave the earth in order to begin our journey, to begin our work. But we cannot possibly stay there if we hope to truly fulfill our heart's desires—we have to come back to earth and breathe. For many, this return is too dense—too depressing— too daunting, and their dreams stay in the clouds.

If you want your dreams to have substance, fruition, and the power to touch others, there is simply no alternative than to put your feet on the ground and start going. Start with anything—one insignificant thing you've been putting off. One phone call you've meant to make. Clean out a closet. Set up a table and finish a project. Send a friend a book you love. Anything! Just start the wheels in motion. Small accomplishments and reaching out provide the momentum that carries you to more connections and steps that lead down your path.

Nugget of Hope

If you have built castles in the air, your work need not be lost; that is where they should be. Now put foundations under them.

—Henry David Thoreau.

Enjoyment

I asked God for all things that
I may enjoy life;
God gave me life that I may
enjoy all things.

—unknown

Not what we have, but what we enjoy, constitutes our abundance. In the Philippines, it is customary, when a guest compliments a hostess on an item in her home, for the

hostess to give the guest that item. The enjoyment the giver and receiver experience is of more value than the object. The feeling of true abundance comes not from ownership of objects but the ability to share and give.

So often, our possessions become the only priority in our lives. We expect that we will find enjoyment from our abundance of "things." Yet, we can have so much that we actually enjoy so little. When I was married, I received a beautiful set of china. In the past fourteen years of owning that china, I've used it twice. My friend, who was born in the Philippines, lives by this rule: If you don't use everything you own, then it's not worth having.

Simplicity is the seasoning of true enjoyment. If we simplify our lives and our possessions to include only enough to completely enjoy, how much more abundance we would experience! Learn to release the objects you don't need and enjoy the space you find. There was once a Carpenter who had very little in the way of material goods— yet he possessed so much.

Nugget of Hope

Those who live Wisdom experience real enjoyment; inner peace, fullness of joy, and total abundance.

—*Cecil O. Kemp, Jr.*

Honor

Honor is the center of character of
*Wisdom... a **mirror image** of*
*   **the Spirit of God** living inside*
*   and glowing out.*
            —Cecil O. Kemp, Jr.

Within our truths, we find our worth embedded in our honor.

I have learned from my grandparents that there is a time to fight and a time to lay down our weapons and appreciate what we have.

The Holocaust was a delicate subject for my grandparents to discuss. They lost their families, they lost their homes, yet they survived. They refused to lose their spirits. When they left Europe and came to America, they committed their lives to giving in abundance, though they often had little to give.

At my grandmother's funeral, the rabbi spoke of honor and grace. He spoke of my grandmother's courage and ability to share herself with others. My grandparents made a difference in so many lives, and the world has become much sweeter because of their honorable actions.

Honor is the sweet surrender of grace given as a light to others so that they may shine.

Nugget of Hope

A honorable heart leads to honorable action. –Debbie Guthery

Identity

*The **greatness** of an artist or writer does not depend on what he has in common with other writers and artists, but on what he has **peculiar** to himself.*
—Alexander Smith

We all carry tiny bits and pieces of our family and their beliefs, values, insights, and talents. These are inherited from the stories that are told or the creations that are shared. Gathering together all of these little pieces, we find an identity of our very own—our own style and understanding. When we discover ourselves, we learn how we "fit" into this life and begin to establish a foundation upon which we can build. That's when we grow.

We all have a fire within us waiting to be shared. Our individuality reveals our footprints of design. Allow yourself the freedom to be who you are and who you are meant to be.

Life is our canvas, and each of us is encouraged to create our own image. With delight in your heart's desires, you will unveil your greatest treasures.

● **Nugget of Hope**
The most important journey is inside, finding there our unique purpose and place!

—*Cecil O. Kemp, Jr.*

Conscience

*Let your **soul guide you***
upon your way.
—*Sting*

I am who I am, because of all that
surrounds me.

Pursue your dreams wisely and
honestly, and taste your success for a lifetime to come. Along
our dream journeys we meet people who teach and influence
us. It is important that we keep our values in our pockets
and our vision clear, so that we can determine the wisdom of
those lessons and that influence. When we then come to a
fork in the road, a place of decision, we have the resources to
make wise choices.

Pinocchio was one of my favorite storybook characters when

I was growing up. He wanted more than anything to become a real boy. The challenges he faced along his way almost cost him his life, and his father, Geppetto, his heart. He was saved by the unconditional love he expressed for his father, by unselfish action, and by "letting his conscience be his guide."

When we stay focused on the Principles of Wisdom, we realize that we can find support in our faith, our values, our families, and the voice from within. Then our dreams will be successful, guided in the ways of Hope and Wisdom.

Nugget of Hope
Choices that move us in a wise spiritual direction always lead us to greater peace, joy, happiness, freedom, and knowledge.

—*Cecil O. Kemp, Jr.*

Commitment
Commitment

The need for devotion to something outside ourselves is even more profound than the need for companionship.
—*Ross Parmenter*

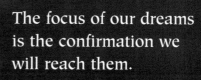

The focus of our dreams is the confirmation we will reach them.

There are no boundaries to hold me now,

my limits—they soar above the ground.

I see no fear, for faith's by my side

and the thorns that once clutched me have withered
and died.

With the wind at my back and the sun on my cheek,

there's no river to cross that is too deep.

I am blessed with confidence, I am surrounded in love.

I am focused on the gifts from heaven above.

I am who I am, and I know my desires

For my dreams are waiting, and my heart is on fire.

Nugget of Hope

*When our lives are committed to fulfillment of eternal
purpose, we achieve our waking dreams and sleeping hopes.*

—*Cecil O. Kemp, Jr.*

Staying True

Staying True

*Our duty to God is to make of ourselves the
most perfect product of divine incarnation
that we can become. This is possible only
through the pursuit of worthy ideas.*

—Edgar White Burrill

Believe, pray, hope, dream, and let faith take you
by the hand. When we pursue our dreams and ideas,
we need to follow these guidelines:

- Be true to yourself.

- Be true to those who share their lives with you.

- Be true to those who come into your life.

- Be honest about your dreams.

When we lose sight of these guidelines, we often lose everything. When my ex-husband and I fell into a small amount of fame, we were so caught up in the attention from strangers that we forgot how to give each other the attention we needed. We were neither true to ourselves nor true to each other; we lost sight of the dreams we shared.

If we follow the guidelines, and love unconditionally along the way, our dreams will never end.

Nugget of Hope
Relationship excellence and success occurs as each party in a relationship is respectful, dutiful, and accountable.

—Cecil O. Kemp, Jr.

Reality

Reality surpasses imagination; and we see, breathing, brightening, and moving before our eyes, sights dearer to our hearts than any we ever beheld in the land of sleep.
—*Johann Wolfgang von Goethe*

Innocence through a child's eyes is a reality we soon forget. Children are wonderful with their bold insights, keen powers of observation, and sometimes abrasive truths. We can learn from our children, who see people as individuals rather than representatives of a whole group, who accept others with openness, who shine with the light of innocence and honesty.

nocence through a child's eyes is a

The moment we learn that physical reality has limits we freeze in our steps and begin to believe that is Truth. In this physical reality, we have certain standards set for us which can erode our self-confidence to see our way clearly. But we do not have to choose this way of seeing.

The word "reality" comes from the roots "thing" (res) and "think" (revi). "Reality" means the "things you think." Change what "things" you wish to think on, and you've changed your reality!

We can decide for ourselves to follow Wisdom's Path in how we feel, what we think, how we should act, and where our imagination takes us. Wise thought and action can get us back on track!

We can determine our own reality to create a place where we can plant our seeds, care for our spirits, and reap the prosperous harvest of our dreams.

Nugget of Hope
Highest reality is spiritual truth, understood and applied via the heart skill of Wisdom.

—*Cecil O. Kemp, Jr*

ity we soon forget.

Actions

Morality regulates the acts of man as a private individual; honor, his acts as a public man.

—Esteban Echeverria

Years ago, I worked in a credit union at a local television station. I had the opportunity to get my hands into production and writing, and I was in heaven. I wanted to start a project that would make a difference, so I began creating a complicated special that I was determined to have televised.

My goal was to create awareness about a small charity that grants wishes to children who are seriously ill or have life-threatening diseases. I invited the children served by that charity to the station to be involved with the production. Because the show would be aired a week before Christmas, the production was complete with Santa Claus and gifts.

I did not anticipate how much joy this effort would bring me, or the silent praise I would receive from the children's excitement as they played and sang and laughed.

Honorable actions arise from honorable dreams that create joy for others.

Nugget of Hope

Our creeds and slogans may be true and wise, but the lessons others learn from us are by observing what we do.
—Cecil O. Kemp Jr.

Belief

Belief

All things are possible for
one who believes.
—*St. Bernard of Clairvaux*

Beliefs carry us beyond our day-to-day
expectations to places where anything is possible.
Beliefs answer our questions and connect our hearts to
our souls. When everything falls apart in our lives, it is
difficult to believe. At times like
that, we need to clean the scraps
off of our plates—the things that cloud
or interfere with our beliefs—and begin
again, ready to be filled with new and
exciting flavors.

I remember times in my life when I had so little left to give and so little room to believe. It would have been much easier to pull the blankets up over my face and turn the lights out than to face my problems. But the faith and beliefs I held so deeply in my soul would not let me. I am compelled— sometimes at my own amazement—to go on and renew my dreams.

There is an old saying that you can take the heart of a man, but you will never steal his soul. The soul holds our beliefs, and with belief there is always room for faith. We are constantly tested in our beliefs and faith, but, as my mother always told me, God gives us only what we can handle and he never leaves our side.

Nugget of Hope
Let your dreams show you what you believe.

Courage

Great things are done more through
courage than through wisdom.
—German proverb

Courage is the strength to eliminate walls, visible and invisible, that confine us. Half of finding our courage lies in acknowledging our desires and the rest in defining our motivations. Courage means we eliminate the excuses, leave the safety of the ledge, and fly with faith that we will be supported by the Spirit of God. Then, we will have no walls to confine us, no limits to bind us, and plenty of room to grow.

My brother-in-law was in a serious accident several years ago. He was expected to die. He lost mobility in his legs and partially in his arms and fingers. He uses a wheelchair, but his courage is unlimited. At the time of the accident, he had one daughter and another baby on the way. He loved them so much, that he determined to live and to live well, to the best of his ability. It has been thirteen years since my brother-in-law's accident, and his courage has never deserted him.

Nugget of Hope
Courage is grace under fire.
—Author Unknown

Patience

There are times when God asks nothing of His children except silence, patience, and tears.
—Charles Seymour Robinson

Sometimes when we need patience most, it is most difficult to find.

I came to a point in my life when it seemed I was caught in a whirlwind of chaos. On my knees, every night, I prayed to God to send me patience. But the more I prayed, the more chaotic my life became.

I talked with a friend about what was happening in my life, and how I was frustrated that God had not helped me find the patience I had prayed for. He laughed sympathetically when I told him about my predicament and then explained to me that God had heard me loud and clear. "God is teaching you patience by giving you chaos. If you learn to handle a truckload of messes, you have not only learned patience, you have mastered it."

That night, when I was on my knees, I thanked God for his blessings and prayed for peace. I learned to let go and let Wisdom be my guide.

Nugget of Hope
They also serve who only stand and wait.

—John Milton

Chances

How many chances do you think we get in a lifetime?

Many years ago, before cars, computers, and airplanes, there lived a holy man. This man devoted his life to God. One night it began to rain. It rained for days and days, but the man continued to sit quietly on a rock praying to God to be saved. Some men arrived on horseback and urged the holy man to jump on and ride away with them. "No," the man said, "God will take care of me." So the horsemen left. The waters rose, and the man continued to pray. Then a large boat appeared, and the boat's captain yelled, "Jump on, and we'll take you to safety." "No," said the man again, "God will provide." The waters continued to rise until the man was swallowed up and drowned. When the holy man reached the pearly gates, he faced the Lord, and asked, "Why did you not save me?" And the Lord replied, "I sent you men on horseback and in a boat, and you denied both."

The principles of Wisdom can help us to take advantage of our chances when they arise and to make wise choices in our actions.

Chances may be God's way of helping us along. If you are dreaming wisely, you should expect His help. Chances may be overlooked, but they are always there waiting to be discovered.

Nugget of Hope
When fortune calls, quick!—offer her a chair!
—*Jewish saying*

Live to please God,
and He will Breathe on thee
His peace.
—F.B. Meyer

and

Don't Forget
to Breathe

Breathing

Breathe on me, Breath of God,
Fill me with life anew.
—Edwin Hatch

As I fall to my knees and call out Your name, I feel You breathe through me.

There are times in our lives when all we can do is throw our arms up in the air and plop down on the ground in exhaustion. I call this breathing time.

We live in a

high-tech, fast-paced, and extremely busy society. We can't slow down enough to catch up with ourselves. Often we are so busy chasing things, we haven't taken the time to understand or learn why.

I am the type of person who never reads directions on packages. I tear into them and guess how the contents work, and most of the time they end up in the attic. Haste prevents me from accomplishing tasks. Most of us have mental "attics" filled with treasures—tasks that we ignored or that we were too frustrated to finish. It is important that we understand why those things were meaningful to us in the first place. We must take the time to slow down, even stop, and breathe. This is not wasting time. This is taking time, using time, to think, rest, reflect, regroup, and follow through.

Nugget of Hope

Let us not go faster than God. It is our emptiness and our thirst that He needs, not our plenitude.

—Jacques Maritain

Loneliness

At the innermost core of all loneliness is a deep and powerful yearning for union with one's lost self.
—Brendon Francis

Many people equate being alone with loneliness, even though they are not the same. A person can feel lonely in a crowded room—or, perfectly content with no one else present.

Loneliness is a longing for companionship, for someone to share our dreams and to reassure us that our dreams will lead us along a wise path. We are most vulnerable when we are faced with sharing something as personal as our dreams.

Our dreams are a part of us, and we want to protect them from ridicule and condemnation. This can lead us to withdraw and become lonely, unsure if our dreams are "good enough," unsure if we can risk sharing them with others.

I've learned that if we share our fear of inadequacy, chances are others will share their hopes, fears, and dreams, too. We can tear down the invisible walls that keep us separated from others and from our own inner peace. When we find that inner spiritual peace, loneliness becomes a temporary state— resting time to breathe and meditate.

I face myself each day and I say, God is here with me, smiling.

Nugget of Hope

Treasure loneliness, as alone time with God. Hear, meditate, and refuel your spirit's hopes and dreams with the Spirit of God's fire and wind.

—*Cecil O. Kemp, Jr.*

Difficulty

Difficulties are God's errands, and when we are sent upon them, we should esteem it a proof of God's confidence. —Henry Ward Beecher

Blessed are our burdens, and the strengths we discover from them. If the world were meant to be given to us on a silver platter, we would have all been born with golden forks in our hands.

Look at your successes, then look at all you have had to go through to attain each one. I would have to say I would not change one single thing in my life, good or bad. Each obstacle was a learning experience that made me who I am today.

When I lost contact with my father, I was devastated. It took many years before I understood that I could not change the situation, but had to grow from it. I loved my father dearly; for some reason, we were not meant to be together then. During our eighteen-year separation of trials, tears, and triumphs, I learned that time moves on, as do we. When the opportunity came to reconnect, we grasped it. My first conversation with my father following the separation lasted only fifteen minutes; a month later, our second conversation lasted an hour, as we worked toward rebuilding our relationship.

Difficulties are the beasts of burden. Learn from them, grow from them, and discover a new strength with in them.

◉ **N**ugget of **H**ope
Difficulties birth inner landmarks,
teaching and changing us for the better.

—*Cecil O. Kemp, Jr.*

Frustration

There seem **times** when one can neither help oneself nor anyone else to find what **we are all in search** of, and it seems impossible to submit or acquiesce. I, as you know, have been

in this frame of mind, and can only say that one does go on, though it seems **impossible**. The only way, I think, is to do whatever comes to one, as quietly and fully as one can.

—A. C. Benson

Upon our travels through life, we often find ourselves circling about going nowhere. Perhaps we need to rest a while.

I flew to Los Angeles several years ago to meet with an advertising agency about some children's books I had written. The gentleman I met with was kind enough to treat me to lunch. We spent hours together, discussing dreams and ambitions. I told him of my frustrations with the publishing companies who would neither read my manuscripts nor give me the time of day.

He empathized with my frustration, and told me something that I will never forget: "When you feel the tension squeeze the back of your neck and you want to retire from all the struggling, hang on to the rope that you've climbed and rest a while, because your dream is just an arm's length away."

Walls can be torn down, mountains can be climbed, and dreams can survive, as long as faith is by your side and in your soul.

Nugget of Hope
Wisdom Poise is calmness in the midst of the storms or the "doldrums" of life and is key to conquering life's daily frustrations.

—Cecil O. Kemp, Jr.

Dedication

God *is in the details.*
—*Albert Einstein*

When we dream big dreams, it's easy to trivialize the basics of human life—the details, the tedious obligations that just don't bring the same joy that dreaming does. However, the Wisdom-filled spirit is asked to bring the same Honor and sense of purpose to all aspects of life—we are asked to be

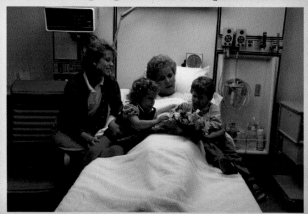

dedicated not just to our grand desires, but to this life that we were given. And this happens to include our health, our finances, our loved ones, our obligations, our parenting, our community.

Just as we breathe every day, we accomplish at least one thing in our waking hours. It could be as small as making breakfast, or as large as saving someone's life. We may not do one thing today that we feel pertains to our dreams. That's OK. Approach all tasks with a wise heart and a desire to do them well. Create for yourself a spirit of dedication in all things.

Dedication is loyalty, to yourself and to your direction. It's knowing how you feel, where you want to go, and what you're willing to do to get there. It's about choice and freedom, experience and growth. It's a place where you believe that anything's possible and dreams are alive.

Dedication is a promise wrapped up in the attention of our hearts.

Nugget of Hope
I pledge with each passing of the sun, to love myself, to love and accept the people around me, and to go to sleep every night knowing I made someone smile.

—*Debbie Guthery*

Learning

learning
learning

> The foundations of learning are:
> **seeing** much, **suffering** much, and
> **studying** much.
> —Catherall

Open a book and discover endless horizons. Open the door to a bookstore and discover—everything! Look at the many books stacked on the shelves. Revel in how many topics you can choose from and how many people have written about anything and everything.

My fiancé and I love to go to a certain bookstore that has a small café on the second floor. I can sit in that café for hours, enjoying the incredible menu and the fantastic atmosphere, surrounded by the books I love. But a bookstore holds more than books and intellectual knowledge: the people who buy the books and the people who sell them bring their own "mini-stories" to the aisles.

We cannot grow in spirit without first mastering its flight; we cannot see without opening our doors; we cannot suffer without taking chances; and we cannot learn without living our dreams.

Almost all valuable learning comes from experiences. When we choose books wisely, we exchange our time for the benefits of other peoples' learning experiences. Books remind us that life is a grand adventure.

Nugget of Hope
Heart smarts is learning life's lessons, retaining that Wisdom in the heart.

—*Cecil O. Kemp, Jr.*

Expression

Expression

> *But true expression, like th'
unchanging sun, Clears and improves whatever
it shines upon; It gilds all objects,
but it alters none.*
>
> —*Pope*

Dance in the clouds and sound trumpets
towards heaven's stars.

Communication, spoken and
unspoken, can sometimes be the most
precious gift we share with one
another. I would like to
share a poem that I
wrote in my diary
several months ago.

*Dance in the clouds and sound
trumpets towards heaven's stars.*

Be still my heart as heaven breathes,

where dreams come true and faith decrees,

in silence pure as angel's wings

I hold my soul in timeless peace.

There is no one interpretation of this poem, because each of us, as a unique being, appreciates life in a different way. We reach within ourselves to discover what we see, feel, and understand. We bring different insights, based on our own experience, to the poem. My college literature professor asked me to interpret a poem she had just recited. I did as she asked, and she quickly interrupted me, objecting to my interpretation. I have learned since then that the most productive interpretation of life—or poetry—is not intellectual, but rather, heartfelt.

Expression is our breath against a mirror, a dream of our own reflection.

Nugget of Hope
Inspired and guided by the Spirit to live Truth, our lives express true excellence.

—Cecil O. Kemp, Jr.

Sharing

When we share—
that is poetry in the prose of life.
—Sigmund Freud

To share is to nurture. To nurture is to grow. But without the sun's rays or the rain's tears, there is no flower.

I used to work in a local bank in Nashville. It was one of the best jobs I have ever had because my co-workers and I became a family. The service to our customers was impeccable and the people I met there became lifetime friends.

Marie, who was probably in her late sixties, came into the bank with her husband several times a week to conduct business. After her husband died, she desperately needed someone to help her with her affairs. I offered to help, and Marie and I became close.

I did my best to care for Marie until her death, even attending to small things like cleaning, washing dishes, running errands, etc. Near the end, she was very ill and rarely spoke. One day when I went to her side, she whispered quietly into my ear, "You are my guardian angel." She died two days later. I have no doubt that, since then, Marie has never left my side. Now I, too, have a guardian angel.

There is no gift greater than the gift of sharing, be it as simple as a smile or an eternity of commitment. We all have something to share. Ideas are merely the seeds, sharing is the nourishment for growth.

Nugget of Hope
Wisdom chooses to honor and serve others, by sharing ourselves.

—Cecil O. Kemp, Jr.

Sacrifice

Without sacrifice there is no resurrection. Nothing grows and blooms save by giving. All you try to save in yourself wastes and perishes.

—André Gide

It's difficult sometimes to see how blessed we are by the sacrifices we make. Although those sacrifices do not always seem best for us, we almost always learn and grow from them. Without sacrifice, there is no victory.

I am in awe of the Bible story about Abraham

who was asked to sacrifice his son, Isaac, as a sign of his love and devotion to God. When God saw that Abraham was obediently following his request, he stopped the sacrifice and blessed Abraham. Abraham learned that he was so committed to his faith, he was willing to give the ultimate sacrifice—his son's life.

During my life as a single mom, I have learned a lot about sacrifice. Most of my dreams were put on hold, and I accepted some limitations on what I could do. By giving up a little for my son's sake, I now have a son who is confident, loving, and intelligent. I can still pursue my dreams, and because of my sacrifices, I have raised a son who honors his own heart and can soar with his own dreams.

Life is constantly changing, as are we. We gather as we grow and experience. Over time, we learn to make wise choices about what we keep and what we leave behind, hoping someday we see a tree where a seed was left behind. How precious are the gifts given with invisible price tags attached.

Nugget of Hope

Nothing that you have not given away will ever really be yours —C. S. Lewis

PASSING ON
PASSING ON

To every thing there is a season, and a time to every purpose under heaven.

—King Solomon

My grandmother was a vibrant, good-hearted, and enchanting woman. She was the magic of my childhood, and I loved her dearly. During one of our last visits, we went through old pictures of her family. One by one, she gave life to each photograph, to the strangers and the places I had longed to visit.

She packed them into a box and asked me to take them. "Debbie," she said, "we have one life to live, so

All the flowers of tomorrows are in the seeds of today

much to share, and very little time to do what we are sent here to do. My time here is almost complete. You must remember these stories, tell your children, and help me to live in the light of your memories, just as my grandmother did for me. It is my time to go and your resistance to letting me go will only leave me miserable in my shell. God has given me treasures to pass on to you. Write about them and carry them always in your heart."

My grandmother died last year. I had trouble letting her go, but I realized it was time for me to say goodbye. Unanchored fears leave limitless boundaries, but I have the pictures and stories to ground me.

Nugget of Hope
All the flowers of all the tomorrows are in the seeds of today.

—*Chinese Proverb*

Letting Go

To grow, *we must heal*
and to heal, we must let go.
—Cecil O. Kemp, Jr.

Letting go of the past is by far the hardest thing to do. We hold all of our experiences close to our hearts and sometimes long to bring them back. But the past is like a match that burns brightly, then slowly fades out until it glows only in memory.

There are things in my past I've had difficulty letting go of: my parents' divorce, my divorce, the loss of a child, and the loss of my grandparents. But I have come to realize that if I continue to mourn the past, I forget to live in the present, and the future becomes like that burned-out match, the wind carrying its smoke into oblivion.

We grow from our experiences, and we learn many wise lessons from past events. But we live in the present, and there's a light on today. Bring your pictures, your memories, and your passions with you. Visit the ones that make you smile or bring you wisdom. Set the others silently upon the smoke, for the wind to carry them away.

Nugget of Hope
Negative thoughts are best left aside when we're trying to fly.   *–Debbie Guthery*

Depression

> Nothing is **miserable** *unless* **you** *think it so.*
>
> —*Boethius*

The winds of change pick us up, whirl us around and leave us dizzy upon our feet. This is when we race home, seeking sanctuary in fear of the unknown.

It is normal to have times in our lives when we feel like crying, surrendering to fear, or just plain doing nothing. A friend of mine calls common depression "the direct line from God." He says we can truly humble ourselves when we are at our worst, and that the tears that stain our cheeks are the acknowledgment that God is near.

I am most effective at writing in my journal during these periods. Not only does writing help me to discover what is making me feel depressed, but it also allows me to resolve the problems. If we realize why we are down in the dumps, we can bring our depression into the light, find peace in our time of contemplation, and fire our engines back up. We can take the time we need to rest and think— and then we can fly again.

☙ Nugget of Hope

When you are depressed is a great time to listen to your heart. Meditate on its messages.

—*Cecil O. Kemp, Jr.*

Defiance

Come one come all,
this rock shall fly,
from its firm base
as soon as I.
—Sir Walter Scott

Many of us have experienced times when we thought life should go our way or no way. Challenge brings us back to reality; it tests our strength and abilities. Challenge breeds knowledge. Defiance lures defeat.

Defiance is a falsehood. It is something we do to test others' feelings towards us. There is a point in our journey, usually when we are trying to grow, where we either must challenge or defy a position.

Defiance is dangerous. We are usually defiant when we become desperate. We may be willing to sacrifice anything to gain control of a situation—the people we love, our neighbors, and even ourselves. When we lose our perspective, we lose our direction and, sometimes, our faith. But we can choose to approach our difficulties realistically and with Wisdom. Then, we remember to breathe, and we can see clearly what frustrates us.

Defiance comes only with defeat. By using our frustrations as an impetus to wise action, we can use this challenge to reach new heights in our dreams.

Humble your heart to appease your soul. Breathe in, breathe out, and remember, we all are able to fly.

Nugget of Hope
Defying defiance, living Truth, is a wise and honorable inner foundation for greatness.

—Cecil O. Kemp, Jr.

Tranquility

The fountain of tranquility is within ourselves; **let us keep it pure.**
—Phocian

The peak of creativity is formed on the edge of our peace.

This was written in my journal after a terrible day at work and a stressful dinner with a client:

I often take drives to clear my head, and I usually end at the water's edge, where the sights and sounds blanket me in serenity. It's quiet here as the waters climb upon the shore and hush the sands beneath them. The ducks clamor and squawk, recounting the events of the day. So many come to the water's edge as if they heard You whisper to them to do so.

I often dream of You, as you dip Your brush into the many colors of the world and stroke it so delicately against the bluest skies, filling them with pastels. As You dip your brush again, You release a fragrance of pines, rain, and honeysuckle. I savor all that You offer, and I am humbled that I may be the guest of Your silent design.

Tranquility is as subtle as the wind, but its brilliance shines upon contemplation. Rest your mind, hear the beating of your heart, and breathe in tranquility as you gather its strength.

Find the peace within you, undisturbed by worry.

ourselves; let us keep it pure

🌀 **N**ugget of **H**ope

Inner spirituality and peace are the passageway and reservoir of inner tranquility.

—*C e c i l   O .   K e m p ,   J r .*

Healing
Healing
Healing

When a door of happiness closes
another door opens;
but often we look so long
at the door that closed,
that we do not see
the one that has been
opened for us.

—Helen Keller

For all that we see, encounter, behold,

For all that we feel both bitter or bold,

For all that is given, or taken from grasp,

For all that we live both present and past,

For all of these gifts from heaven above,

upon wings of angels and graced with love,

Is all of the wisdom we need each day

until angels come forth and carry us away.

Wounds that are deep and difficult to heal grace the heart
with so much more to give. Breathe. Inhale the pain and
gently begin again.

Nugget of Hope
*Healing begins with spiritual wholeness. Inner healing is
seen outward in improved behavior and performance.*

—*Cecil O. Kemp, Jr.*

Hope

Hope is a thing with feathers / that perches on the soul, / And sings the tune without the words, / And never stops at all
—Emily Dickinson

If you watch the children's tears disappear, you can see the very seed of hope blossoming upon their cheeks and gracefully dancing into their eyes.

When A Child Prays

I heard a whisper behind closed doors
the simple words uttered were blessed and pure
and something happened that miraculous day
when I heard a child pray.

Sparrows gathered on the windowsill
and the earth's sweet chatter became quiet and still
And heaven's arms embraced oceans and hills
when I heard a child pray.

Angels began dancing on the silver clouds
and nations laid down weapons and quietly bowed
And the souls that had been lost were suddenly found
When I heard a child pray.

Something miraculous happened that day
in the heart of a child the Lord came to stay
reminding us all in a special way
to listen...when a child prays.

Hope is the breath of a
child. We all have a
child within us.
For every breath,
for every wish,
there is a dream
called hope.

Nugget of Hope
Be a river of Hope, not a dam.

—Cecil O. Kemp, Jr.

Inspire Others

One loving heart
sets another on fire.
— *Augustine*

The most important
Breathing we can ever
experience is to Inspire—
literally "to breathe into"—
another person, just as God
breathes into us.

Michelangelo was once
assisted in his work by
a marble hewer who,
by following

instructions—"cut this away... level that... polish here"—was amazed to find that he had created a splendid marble figure. "What do you think of it?" asked Michelangelo. "I think it's fine." replied the man, "and I am much obliged to you. Through your instruction I have discovered a talent that I did not know I possessed."

If you have dreamed wisely, you have chosen a path that gives you great joy and fulfillment and at the same time offers a service or joy to others. There will come a time along your journey when you must pass on your passion, your spirit, your talent—perhaps as a mentor or teacher. Perhaps as a parent or grandparent. Perhaps as an artist whose work reaches and opens eyes and hearts, transferring the passion and beauty of your work into the soul of the observer.

And so the dream continues...

Nugget of Hope
The beauty seen is partly in him who sees it.

—*Bovee*

Freedom

Allow yourself the Freedom
to be who you are
and **who you were meant to be.**
—Debbie Guthery

Freedom is the right to choose:
the right to create for yourself
the alternatives of choice.
—Archibald MacLeish

I taste the wind on my lips and fly upon its current. Why bind my feet, when I have finally found my wings?

Walk among your dreams. Know there is nothing that can hold you back. Take chances. Learn how. Breathe in, breathe out. Express yourself. Live well. Live honestly. Do. Notice

In our inner sanctuary, we breath in the sp

Cecil O. Kemp, Jr.

small blessings. Celebrate all creation. Smile often, give much, help willingly. Swing on a swing, splash in a fountain. Keep good memories, learn from the bad ones. Harness the wind, release your spirit. Walk with truth, think with your heart. Laugh, hug, take care of the child within. Talk to animals, talk to strangers, talk to children. Thank the people

in your life for being part of your life. Live with love, live with Hope, live with Honor, and live with Wisdom.

Remember to dream big, dream wisely—and don't forget to breathe.

⦿ Nugget of Hope

In our inner sanctuary, we breathe in the Spirit of God... [we] wisely dream big dreams. —C e c i l   O.   K e m p,   J r.

of God...we wisely dream big dreams.

ABOUT THE PUBLISHER

The Wisdom Company (TWC) began in 1983. Its founder, Cecil O. Kemp, Jr., grew up on a small rural farm and married his childhood sweetheart, Patty. Their two children have each made the Kemps doting Grandparents. Cecil graduated college in 1971, immediately passed the CPA exam, and worked with one of the world's largest accounting firms. He became Chief Financial Officer of a publicly held stock company at 23, and its COO before 30. Since 1982, the Kemps have owned many successful businesses, including TWC.

TWC's purpose is Sharing The Hope of Wisdom. Its inspirational and character education materials all express the principles, values, and priorities of spiritual Truth—as expressed in Cecil's acclaimed book, Wisdom Honor & Hope which points to The Inner Path to True Greatness. TWC offers two series of Collectible Gift Books, The Hope Collection and The Wisdom Series. Our aim in each book is to encourage the reader and to share:

- A renaissance of the individual lifestyle shaped by Wisdom

- The way toward true excellence and lasting success

- The Inner Path of integrity in daily living, thinking and decision making

- The joy of achieving and maintaining Inner Peace, the wellspring of true happiness and satisfaction